Hypergamy

Who do they choose?
What do you do to get them to choose you?

Phillip A. Johansen

Editorial Anuket

Contents

Introduction

Introduction

If we start from the morphological meaning, the word hypergamy is composed of 'hyper', which denotes superiority or excess, and 'gamy', which comes from Greek and provides the meaning of union or marriage. Thus, the term hypergamy is used to describe the tendency of an individual to seek partners who are perceived as having a higher social, economic, or educational status. Although this behavior can be observed in both men and women, the motivations and how it manifests are different between genders, due to a combination of biological, cultural, and social factors.

Hypergamy vs. Hypogamy

Hypergamy is the practice of marrying someone from a social or cultural group of equal or higher status than one's own and occurs predominantly when women marry a man with a higher educational, economic, or social level. In contrast, hypogamy occurs when women marry men of lower status (or the reverse: when men marry women of higher status), although this practice is less common in cultures where women have fewer rights.

Both concepts are part of the broader sociological discourse on mate selection, highlighting the dynamics of social mobility and marital choices.

Homogamy

Homogamy refers to the tendency of individuals to marry others who have similar characteristics, such as educational level, social class, and ethnicity. This phenomenon occurs in stratified societies, where couples often feel more comfortable seeking life partners who occupy similar positions within the social structure.

While hypergamy and hypogamy focus on the rise or fall of social status, homogamy emphasizes similarity and social dynamics within relationships.

Cultural Hypergamy

Cultural Hypergamy refers to relationships between individuals from different cultural backgrounds who are faced with the complexities of combining traditions and values. When partners share a deep appreciation for each other's sensibilities, they engage in a multicultural relationship, enriching their lives through shared experiences such as language, food, and music.

This aspect emphasizes that Hypergamous relationships are not based solely on financial status but can also be based on emotional and intellectual connections.

Hypergamy in Women

Traditionally, female Hypergamy has been a recurring theme in the study of evolutionary psychology. From a biological perspective, women prioritize the security and resources a partner can provide. This tendency is attributed to the evolutionary need to ensure the survival and well-being of their future children. Therefore, women often value qualities such as:

Economic stability: A man's ability to provide for and maintain the family is a key factor in many cultures.

Social Status: Women may seek out men who have a higher status in society, as this can translate into a better quality of life and opportunities for offspring.

Maturity and Leadership: Men who are perceived as natural protectors or leaders are often attractive, due to their ability to manage difficult situations.

Culturally, the Hypergamous woman seeks out someone who gives her a sense of progress, and elevates her to a higher level, whether socially, emotionally, or financially. This does not mean that all women pursue this type of relationship, but the tendency is documented and frequently seen in traditional romantic dynamics.

Hypergamy in Men

Although less discussed, Hypergamy can also occur in men, but it manifests itself differently. Men, from an evolutionary perspective, tend to seek out partners who show signs of fertility and youth, as this ensures healthy offspring. However, when it comes to status or resources, men often opt for hypogamous relationships (where the partner has a lower status) rather than hypergamous ones. The characteristics they value include:

<u>Physical attractiveness:</u> In most cultures, men typically seek out women who are perceived as young and physically attractive, as these are indicators of fertility.

<u>Emotional and supportive qualities:</u> Men seek out partners who provide emotional support, understanding, and a stable home environment.

<u>Status symmetry:</u> Although it is more common for men to seek out women with less status or resources, they also look for a certain symmetry in values and life goals.

However, in modern societies, some men also seek out women with high levels of education or professional success, which can be seen as a new form of male hypergamy. This phenomenon has become more visible as women have gained economic and social independence, challenging traditional power dynamics.

Social and Cultural Factors

Hypergamy has been reinforced by centuries of patriarchal structure, where the man was the provider, and the woman depended on her status to access better opportunities. We can cite an example to visualize this situation. Women's suffrage was approved in England in 1928; until then, women were confined to the home, and men were recognized as representatives of the family outside, making decisions for all members (even if some of them did not agree). Therefore, men held the power that women longed for. In many cultures, men are still expected to be the ones who provide economic stability and face adversities that may threaten the family, while women strive to protect and educate the children.

However, in recent decades, this model has begun to change. The increase in gender equality and female economic independence has created a new dynamic, where both men and women have the freedom to choose partners based on different criteria, beyond traditional status. Now, women may choose not to follow Hypergamous guidelines and prioritize emotional, intellectual, or sexual compatibility, while some men are more open to relationships with women with outstanding careers and achievements.

Psychological Factors

The psychology of Hypergamy incorporates elements of self-image and perceived social status. People often evaluate potential partners not only based on their economic status but also on various attributes, such as intelligence and creativity.

Self-esteem plays a key role in this dynamic: those with higher self-esteem may seek out partners they perceive as more desirable, while people with lower self-esteem may settle for partners they consider "safe."

Economic Influences on Relationships

The intersection between economics and relationships raises questions about whether financial status can significantly influence romantic attraction. While the saying "money can't buy love" persists, economic factors frequently affect partner selection in contemporary society, leading to ongoing debates about the role of financial stability in romantic relationships.

Therefore, understanding Hypergamy also requires examining how social pressures and economic considerations influence individuals' decisions in love and partnership.

Key Differences

Biological Motivations: While women tend to focus more on stability and resources, men traditionally seek youth and physical attractiveness.

Social Status: Women generally seek men with a higher or equal status than them, while men do not consider the social status of women as much, preferring physical or emotional attributes.

Role Change: In modern society, roles have begun to blend. Some women seek men for their physical attractiveness or emotional compatibility, while some men value professional success and the status of women.

Hypergamy is a concept that has influenced relationships for centuries, with clear differences between men and women. However, the dynamics are changing, and the evolution of gender roles is transforming the rules of the game. In contemporary societies, where both genders can access economic independence, relationships are becoming more balanced and less dependent on traditional hypergamous structures.

Chapter 1
The Origins of Hypergamy: Biology and Evolution

This chapter explores the evolutionary origin of hypergamy in men and women, explaining how biological differences have shaped preferences in mate choice. We will discuss the female need for security and resources, and the male focus on youth and fertility, providing a scientific basis for understanding current behavior.

Hypergamy, as a mate selection phenomenon, has deep roots dating back to the earliest days of humanity. Before culture, social norms, or digital platforms could influence mate choice, biological instincts for survival and reproduction were the main factors dictating the dynamics between men and women.

Natural and Sexual Selection

To understand the origins of hypergamy, it is crucial to understand the difference between natural selection and sexual selection. Natural selection refers to an individual's ability to survive in its environment, while sexual selection focuses on the characteristics that make an individual attractive as a reproductive partner.

Natural selection influences hypergamous behavior by driving women to seek partners who provide stability and resources, characteristics that can increase the chances of survival of their children. A short, bald man who is the director of a multinational company may be more attractive than an athletic, unemployed, and unambitious young man.

Sexual selection, on the other hand, motivates men to seek partners with characteristics associated with fertility, such as youth and physical health, increasing their chances of passing on genes to the next generation. In this case, the man will prefer a woman in her twenties with a medium education, rather than a woman in her forties with a degree and high status.

Biological Differentiation: Parental Investment

One of the fundamental concepts that explain the differences in mating strategies between men and women is parental investment. In mammalian species, including humans, females invest significantly more time and resources in reproduction than males.

In women, parental investment is considerable. Pregnancy, childbirth, and breastfeeding involve a great expenditure of energy and time, which makes them more selective when choosing a partner. A woman could conceive about 10 children throughout her fertile stage, so she strives to mate with the best man. Evolutionarily, women tend to seek out men capable of providing resources, protection, and stability, ensuring that their parental investment has a greater chance of success.

In men, the parental investment is much lower. He could impregnate a different woman every day, and his fertile stage is much longer than that of women. Due to the ability to reproduce without the need for such a significant physical or temporal investment as that of women, men have historically focused on maximizing the number of offspring, and hence their tendency towards natural polygamy (contact with the greatest number of different females). For this reason, they tend to prefer young and fertile women, who can guarantee healthy offspring.

Female Hypergamy: Security and Resources

From an evolutionary perspective, female Hypergamy is rooted in the search for security and resources. Women, faced with the challenges of raising children in unpredictable and potentially dangerous environments, developed a preference for partners who could offer:

• **Material resources:** Such as food, shelter, and access to goods essential for survival.

• **Physical protection:** Men who could protect themselves and their children from external threats, whether from other humans or predators. It is notable to note that in ancient or medieval times where fighting was primarily hand-to-hand, the strongest man was the most desired. Today, due to technology, women desire healthy-looking, self-grooming men over bodybuilders, who are seen as self-centered and with extreme and unhealthy eating habits. On the other hand, women admire a firm, masculine backside, perhaps because it was what ancient hunters possessed, who had to run miles to catch their prey.

• **Social status:** Higher status generally indicated that a man had access to better resources and a greater ability to protect his family. This also meant that his children would have greater opportunities for success in the future.

This strategy ensured that women not only chose the most physically attractive men but also those with the characteristics necessary to ensure the survival and well-being of their offspring.

Male Hypergamy: Youth and Fertility

Although the word "hypergamy" is most associated with women, men also show selective tendencies in their mate choices, but these tend to be more oriented toward indicators of fertility than resources or status.

• **Youth:** From an evolutionary perspective, youth is associated with a woman's ability to have multiple children. Men tend to prefer young women because, in terms of reproduction, they offer greater opportunities for having numerous and healthy offspring.

• **Physical attractiveness:** Certain physical characteristics, such as smooth skin, shiny hair, and a curvy body with large breasts and wide hips, are instinctively interpreted as signs of health and fertility. These attributes have been universally desired throughout history, as they indicated a high likelihood of reproductive success.

Culture and Evolution: A Complex Interaction

Hypergamy is deeply influenced by cultural norms and historical practices. In certain societies, particularly in the context of arranged marriages, social position and family lineage are central to choosing a spouse. This social expectation of hypergamy underscores its acceptance and prevalence in specific cultural contexts, further highlighting the importance of economic and social factors in mate selection.

While biology has played a crucial role in shaping mating preferences in men and women, culture has amplified or modified these dynamics at different historical times and social contexts.

<u>Gender roles:</u> Traditional cultures have reinforced gender roles based on these biological inclinations. Women were valued for their youth and reproductive ability, while men were valued for their strength, ability to provide, and leadership.

<u>Marriage as a survival strategy:</u> For much of human history, marriage was not only a union based on romantic love but also an economic and survival strategy. This reinforced hypergamous dynamics, where the woman sought a man of higher status or greater resources.

Over time, these dynamics have evolved along with social changes, but the biological basis of Hypergamy remains evident in many contemporary cultures, albeit camouflaged by modern norms and expectations.

Hypergamy in Modernity: Persistence or Change?

With the advent of modernity, many of the conditions that favored Hypergamy have changed. Access to education, female economic independence, and technological advances have given rise to new dynamics in mate choice. However, many of the basic instincts remain:

Independent and selective women: Even though many women are no longer economically dependent on a man, status is still an important factor in mate selection. The difference is that status can now include factors such as intelligence, education, or professional success.

Men and the attraction to female success: In some cases, modern men may also be attracted to women who display success in terms of social or economic status. This phenomenon challenges traditional models of male hypergamy, which has always preferred women of equal or lower status than him, to develop his masculinity as a protector. However, men have always needed recognition of their value and usefulness, a situation that is difficult when women exercise family leadership.

Hypergamy, in both men and women, has deep roots in our biology and evolution. Although culture and social advances have transformed how we relate to

each other in modern societies, many of the underlying
instincts persist.

Chapter 2
Hypergamy in Women:
Security and Stability

Hypergamy in women understood as the tendency to seek partners with higher social, economic, or educational status, has been widely documented in various cultures and historical contexts. In this chapter, we delve into the roots of this trend, its manifestations in modern society, and how the search for security and stability influences women's mating decisions. We will also examine how changing gender roles and female economic independence are transforming this traditional dynamic.

The Biological Basis of Female Hypergamy

From an evolutionary perspective, female hypergamy has a clear justification: the search for a partner who can provide security and resources to ensure the survival of the woman and her offspring. As we have explained, women, due to their greater parental investment (pregnancy, childbirth, and parenting), tend to be more selective when choosing a partner. This selectivity is guided by the need to ensure that the man can offer constant support and resources in the long term.

Economic stability: In the early stages of human evolution, resources were scarce and difficult to obtain. Men with access to food, shelter, and adequate tools were more attractive to women, as they ensured the survival of both them and their children.

Protection: In an environment filled with threats, from wild animals to tribal conflict, a man's ability to protect his mate and children was also crucial. Women who chose mates with skills to defend themselves and secure territory increased the odds of survival for their offspring.

This selection process was not conscious, but rather a manifestation of deep-seated instincts that evolved to maximize survival and reproductive success. Although societies have changed and access to resources is no longer dependent on physical strength, women continue to display preferences that reflect these ancient evolutionary dynamics.

Hypergamy in Traditional Society

Historically, female Hypergamy has been reinforced by social and economic structures that limited women's independence. For centuries, women depended on men for access to resources, property, and social status. Marriage became a tool to improve women's economic and social position, and it was vital to choose a man with power, influence, or wealth.

Strategic marriages: In many societies, marriage was not a matter of love, but a strategic transaction that allowed families to improve their position in the community. Marriages between lower-class women and men from higher classes or with greater economic power were common, and women's families encouraged these unions to ensure long-term security.

<u>The role of dowry and status:</u> In cultures where dowry played an important role, female hypergamy was more pronounced. Women with higher dowries could aspire to better husbands, while those from humble families sought to rise socially through marriage to men of higher status.

This traditional hypergamous model kept women in a subordinate role, where economic and social security depended largely on choosing a partner who could provide stability.

Influence of technology

The rise of online dating platforms has further transformed hypergamous behaviors by expanding the pool of potential partners. Geographical and social barriers that previously limited partner choice have diminished, allowing people to connect with a wide range of potential partners. This has also led to the development of filtering options based on education, profession, and lifestyle preferences, allowing users to seek out relationships that more closely align with their aspirations.

Hypergamy in Modernity: Independence and New Stability

The 20th century brought with it a revolution in gender roles and economic dynamics. Women gained access to higher education, began to enter the workforce, and eventually achieved economic independence that challenged traditional norms. However, while female Hypergamy has evolved, it remains an observable trend in partner choice.

<u>Economic independence, but with expectations:</u> Today, women are no longer completely dependent on men for resources, giving them greater freedom to choose a partner based on emotional, intellectual, or sexual compatibility. However, studies have shown that even in economically independent women, the preference for men with higher or equal economic status remains prevalent. This is because security and stability, although no longer limited to material things, remain a key factor.

<u>Emotional compatibility and stability:</u> In modernity, the security that women seek in a partner is not only economic but also emotional. Stability in a relationship now includes factors such as emotional support, compatibility in values, and the ability to resolve conflicts maturely. Female Hypergamy, in this sense, has transformed to also include criteria of psychological and relational stability.

This phenomenon reflects a shift in the concept of "security," which has moved from being purely material to include emotional well-being and overall quality of life.

Social Expectations and Hypergamy

Despite advances in gender equality, social expectations still play an important role in Hypergamous dynamics. In many cultures, men are expected to provide or at least be able to match or surpass the economic status of their partners. This social pressure can influence both men and women:

<u>Pressure on women:</u> Although more and more women reject traditional norms, there is still cultural pressure for them to "rise" in socioeconomic status through their partners. This is particularly evident in family and social expectations, where a woman may be seen as successful if her partner has a high status.

<u>The Impact on Men:</u> Men, for their part, feel pressure to live up to these expectations. Those who do not have a high economic status may feel inadequate or less attractive, even if they possess other valuable qualities. This dynamic can create tension in relationships, especially in an era where women are increasingly independent and successful.

The New Hypergamy: Social and Intellectual Status

In contemporary societies, where women have more freedom of choice than ever before, Hypergamy has in some cases shifted toward criteria of social and intellectual status. Women seek not only men with economic resources but also those who have:

<u>Professional success:</u> A man with ambitions, a stable job, and the ability to continue growing in his career is

valued positively, as professional success is associated with stability and progress.

<u>Intellectual ability:</u> Intellectual status, which includes education, cultural level, and emotional intelligence, has become a crucial factor for many women when choosing a partner. As women achieve higher levels of education, they are more likely to seek out men who can hold deep conversations and share intellectual interests.

The Dangers of Hypergamy: Expectations and Realities

While Hypergamy can offer benefits in terms of security and stability, it can also lead to problems when expectations do not align with reality. Some women seeking a Hypergamous partner may face:

<u>Unrealistic expectations:</u> Modern society often presents models of success that are difficult for most men to achieve. This can lead women to search for a "Prince Charming" who, in practice, is difficult to find. These unrealistic expectations can lead to frustration and disillusionment.

<u>Emotional or financial dependence:</u> Even in modern times, some women may fall into the trap of becoming emotionally or financially dependent on a man with greater resources, which can undermine their independence and long-term well-being.

Hypergamy and Feminism

Female Hypergamy and the feminist movement are two concepts that have sparked debate about the dynamics of gender relations. While female Hypergamy refers to the tendency of some women to seek partners who have a higher social, economic, or educational status than their own, feminism is a movement that fights for equal rights and opportunities for women in all areas.

At first glance, it might seem that Hypergamy and feminism are in contradiction. Feminism, especially in its more modern form, advocates for the independence and empowerment of women, suggesting that they should not depend on men to improve their social or economic status. However, some critics point out that certain aspects of Hypergamy are perpetuated despite feminist advances. This can be seen in the social expectation that many women still face to find a partner who will "improve" their position.

From a feminist perspective, hypergamy is sometimes seen as a reflection of historical structural inequalities. Traditionally, women have had fewer economic and social opportunities than men, which encouraged the search for partners with greater resources. Some sectors of feminism consider that, in a completely egalitarian society, hypergamy should disappear, since women would not need to look "upwards" to ensure their well-being.

On the other hand, some critics of feminism argue that the hypergamous phenomenon continues to strengthen, even in societies with feminist advances, suggesting that it has deep roots in human biology or psychology. From this perspective, the instinct to seek security and protection in a partner with higher status may be an evolutionary strategy that transcends social norms.

The relationship between female hypergamy and feminism is complex. While feminism seeks to eliminate the barriers that impede women's independence and individual development, hypergamy seems to continue to influence couple dynamics. This debate invites us to reflect on how much of our relationship decisions are influenced by social norms and how much comes from factors more deeply rooted in human nature.

Female Hypergamy has evolved from its biological roots to adapt to contemporary realities. Although modern women have more choice and freedom than ever before, the search for security and stability remains a predominant factor in partner choices. However, that "security" has taken on new forms, including emotional stability, intellectual success, and compatibility of values. As societal expectations continue to change, Hypergamy will too, reflect the new power and gender dynamics today.

Chapter 3
Hypergamy in Man:
Youth and Beauty

As we have mentioned, when we talk about hypergamy, it usually refers to the phenomenon of women seeking partners with higher socioeconomic status. However, in men, although the behavior does not fit the traditional concept of hypergamy, there are also clear selective preferences. Men tend to show an inclination towards youth and beauty in their partners, factors that from an evolutionary perspective are associated with fertility and reproductive capacity. In this chapter we will explore the motivations behind this inclination, how it has manifested itself throughout history, and how it remains a relevant dynamic today.

The Evolutionary Basis: Youth as a Symbol of Fertility

Like female hypergamy which is based on the search for security and resources, male hypergamy (if you can call it that) is oriented towards the search for signs of fertility and health in a partner. Men have been selected, evolutionarily, to prefer young and physically attractive women, as these attributes indicate greater reproductive capacity.

Youth as an indicator of fertility: Youth, in biological terms, is associated with a woman's peak reproductive capacity. In ancient times, when infant mortality rates were higher and life expectancy was shorter, men who chose young women were more likely to father children who survived to maturity.

<u>Physical attractiveness and health cues</u>: Physical characteristics such as smooth skin, shiny hair, and a favorable waist-to-hip ratio (suggesting good reproductive capacity) were key indicators that a woman was fertile and healthy. These subconscious signals of physical health and fertility allowed men to identify mates who were likely to be more successful in giving birth to healthy children.

In other words, while women historically sought resources and protection in a partner, men sought mates who could ensure the successful transmission of their genes. This generated a strong preference for youth and beauty, which remains present in men in modern societies, although circumstances have changed. That is why it is not surprising that men become emotionally involved with women 10 years younger than them, while society looks with strange eyes at women who frequent men 10 years younger than them, accusing them of "robbing cradles."

Historical Manifestations of Male Hypergamy

Throughout history, men's preference for young and attractive women has been evident in various cultures and contexts. This inclination is not a new phenomenon, but a constant trait that has influenced human relationships over time.

<u>Unions of older men with young women</u>: In many traditional societies, older and more resourceful men

married young women. These marriages not only guaranteed genetic transmission, but also reinforced the social status of the man, who, by uniting with a young and attractive woman, demonstrated his ability to access a fertile and desired partner.

Ideals of female beauty in history: From ancient Greece to imperial China, standards of female beauty have been linked to youth, health, and reproductive capacity. At different times in history, the ideal of female beauty has been represented by young women with proportionate bodies, which denoted fertility and health.

Polygamy and youth: In polygamous societies, it was common for high-status men to have several wives, often younger than themselves. Younger women held a special place in these relationships due to their ability to bear more children and their physical attractiveness.

Male Hypergamy in Contemporary Society

Although societies have evolved and social advances have changed gender dynamics, men's preference for youth and beauty remains an observable phenomenon in modern relationships. However, these preferences have adapted to new cultural and technological realities.

Social media and dating apps: Digital platforms have facilitated access to a wide variety of potential partners, and many men continue to prioritize physical attraction in their decisions. Dating apps, such as

Tinder or Bumble, encourage this trend, as physical attractiveness is the first visible criterion and is often decisive for men when it comes to making a match.

<u>Youth as a status factor:</u> In today's societies, a relationship with a young and attractive woman is still seen as a status symbol for many men. High-profile or economically powerful men are often paired with much younger women, reinforcing the idea that female youth is a desired and valuable commodity. This phenomenon is common in society's elite, from movie stars to successful businessmen.

<u>Cosmetic surgery and beauty standards:</u> In contemporary culture, women also face pressure to maintain their youthful and attractive appearance for longer. The rise of cosmetic surgery, the use of anti-aging products, and the obsession with maintaining a youthful image have been exacerbated by the male preference for youth, which reinforces unrealistic beauty standards.

Differences in expectations of men and women

While female hypergamy tends to focus on status and economic stability, male hypergamy is more focused on physical appearance. This difference in priorities can lead to tensions and misunderstandings in modern relationships, where both men and women look for different things in a partner:

<u>Women and economic expectations:</u> Women, especially those who have achieved economic independence, tend to look for partners who are equal or superior to them

in terms of status, income, or academic achievements. For women, stability remains important, but the search for a partner with higher status may also be influenced by cultural and social expectations.

<u>Men and physical expectations:</u> Men, while valuing intelligence and personality in a partner, often prioritize physical attractiveness in the early stages of a relationship. This can lead to frustration in women who have invested in their personal or professional development, only to feel valued primarily for their appearance.

Youth and Beauty in Male Maturity

The preference for youth also changes as men age. While young men tend to seek partners of their age or slightly younger, older men often prefer significantly younger women. This trend has several explanations:

<u>Access to young partners through status:</u> As men mature and achieve higher economic and social status, they have more access to young, attractive women. This is especially evident in men who reach positions of power or wealth, where their partner's youth becomes a sign of personal success.

<u>Maintaining male vitality:</u> For some men, having a younger partner can be a way to reaffirm their vitality and masculinity. By joining a young woman, these men feel that they are still desirable and capable of attracting partners in their reproductive prime.

This phenomenon can create tensions in relationships between older couples, where the age gap can create differences in expectations, interests, and lifestyles.

It is said that the ideal age difference is 7 years, since, beyond that period, we are talking about different generations that will have little in common. A 30-year-old man is perfect since he has reached his maturity, is clear about his objectives, and works towards them, together with a 23-year-old woman, who is in her golden age (18 to 25), they become a powerful couple.

The Dangers of "Male Hypergamy"

The male preference for youth and beauty is not without negative consequences. In many cases, these expectations can lead to shallow or unsatisfying long-term relationships. Some of the risks include:

Relationships based on superficial appearance: Choosing a partner based almost exclusively on physical appearance can lead to relationships where the emotional or intellectual connection is weak. These often-unsustainable relationships can end when physical attraction wanes or when one partner seeks a deeper connection.

Long-term dissatisfaction: Men who prioritize youth and beauty may find themselves trapped in a constant search for the "perfect" partner, leaving them dissatisfied or unable to maintain long-term relationships. Beauty and youth are temporary, and those who only seek these attributes may experience personal or emotional crises as their partners age or change physically.

<u>Encouraging unrealistic beauty standards:</u> The male preference for youth also reinforces unrealistic beauty standards in women, which can lead to self-esteem issues or body dysmorphia in many women, who feel the pressure to meet impossible expectations.

The Evolution of Male Hypergamy

Although the modern world has changed the rules of the game in terms of relationships and couple dynamics, the male preference for youth and beauty is still a present phenomenon, influenced by evolutionary and cultural factors. However, this trend must also be viewed critically, as ideals of beauty and youth do not always lead to satisfying or healthy long-term relationships. For men, recognizing and balancing these preferences with other values, such as emotional and intellectual compatibility, can be key to building deeper and longer-lasting relationships in an ever-changing society.

Chapter 4
Common mistakes
in the hypergamy dynamic

Hypergamy, in both men and women, is a phenomenon that reflects deep preferences based on biological, social, and cultural factors. However, Hypergamous dynamics can lead to errors and misunderstandings when interpreted or applied in extreme or erroneous ways in modern life. These errors not only affect interpersonal relationships, but can also influence people's self-esteem, expectations, and quality of life. In this chapter, we will delve into the most common errors in Hypergamous dynamics and how they can undermine both romantic relationships and personal well-being.

Criticism and Controversy

Hypergamy has generated significant criticism and controversy over the years, often sparking heated debates about gender dynamics and societal values. In essence, critics argue that Hypergamous behavior reinforces outdated stereotypes, particularly regarding women's motivations in relationships. Some argue that this trend is primarily driven by the pursuit of partners with a higher economic status, calling it superficial searching.

However, proponents of Hypergamy claim that it encompasses a broader range of factors, including compatibility and shared values, rather than focusing solely on wealth.

The discourse around Hypergamy is often polarized, with detractors framing it as an anti-feminist notion, while supporters argue that it can be viewed through a modern feminist lens. Critics suggest that Hypergamy perpetuates the idea that women prioritize financial security over genuine connection, which they claim undermines women's autonomy and complicates dating dynamics.

In contrast, supporters of Hypergamy argue that it reflects informed choice, allowing people to pursue relationships that align with their aspirations and values rather than being limited by traditional gender roles.

Furthermore, some scholars have pointed out that the fear associated with Hypergamy can distort perceptions and create communities that vilify the opposite sex. This fear, which is often rooted in concerns about infidelity and commitment, can lead to generalizations that paint all individuals who engage in Hypergamous behavior as manipulative or unethical.

As such, critics argue that discussions surrounding Hypergamy should focus on fostering mutual understanding rather than perpetuating divisive narratives. The debate is further complicated by the changing nature of relationships in the 21st century, where the motivations behind Hypergamous choices can differ significantly across cultural contexts. Critics argue that contemporary Hypergamy can appear to be a survival strategy rather than a conscious preference, particularly in environments where financial stability is paramount. In contrast, supporters argue that Hypergamy is increasingly viewed as a valid relationship choice that allows people to pursue fulfilling relationships that transcend mere economic considerations.

Ultimately, while Hypergamy continues to generate debate, it remains a multifaceted topic that reflects broader societal changes and individual choices in the realm of romantic relationships.

Partner Idealization Based on Hypergamous Stereotypes

One of the most common mistakes in Hypergamous dynamics is over-idealizing one's partner based on stereotypes. Both men and women can fall into the error of creating an idealized image of the "perfect" partner that fits Hypergamous standards, which can lead to unsatisfying relationships and disappointment.

<u>Women Seeking an Idealized "Provider Man"</u>: Many women, influenced by the Hypergamous paradigm, tend to seek out men who fit an image of an ideal provider, expecting them to be financially successful, have high social status, and can provide security. However, by idealizing a man solely based on his economic status or ability to provide, women can overlook fundamental aspects of the relationship, such as emotional compatibility or the quality of the emotional bond. This can lead to superficial relationships where long-term satisfaction is difficult to achieve.

<u>Men who idealize youth and beauty</u>: Similarly, some men make the mistake of focusing exclusively on youth

and physical beauty when choosing a partner. While these traits are superficially attractive, they do not guarantee a stable, emotionally satisfying relationship in the long term. Men who constantly seek out younger or more attractive women may find themselves trapped in an endless search for a "better fit," undermining their ability to form deep and meaningful relationships.

This type of idealization leads to unrealistic expectations that inevitably lead to frustration when reality does not match the fantasy.

Modern dynamics and cultural perspectives

Contemporary thinkers approach Hypergamy from a variety of angles, often viewing it as an intrinsic aspect of human nature that requires careful management to maintain social stability. The concept is perceived differently in different cultures: in some societies, marriage to a higher-status person is celebrated for financial and social stability, while in others it may be viewed skeptically as opportunism or social advancement.

Furthermore, cultural exchanges brought about by globalization have introduced diverse attitudes toward Hypergamy, complicating its understanding and practice in different societies.

The mistake of basing personal value on the partner

Another common mistake in Hypergamous dynamics is that of measuring personal value based on the status of the partner. Both men and women can fall into the trap of thinking that the quality of their partner (in terms of status, appearance, or achievements) directly reflects their value as individuals. This approach can have profound negative effects on self-esteem and self-perception.

Women who measure their success by the status of their partner: In some cases, women tend to measure their value based on the success or power of their partner. This dynamic is a byproduct of traditional expectations of Hypergamy, where the woman was seen as "elevated" by the social or economic position of her partner. Although women today have more independence, some still feel pressure to have a partner who "validates" their success. This can lead to unbalanced or even toxic relationships being accepted, if the man has a high status, but does not offer real emotional support or respect.

Men who define their masculinity by their partner's attractiveness: On the other hand, some men make the mistake of measuring their masculinity or personal success based on how attractive their partner is. Constantly seeking external approval through a woman's physical appearance can divert attention from what matters in a relationship: emotional connection, mutual respect, and reciprocal support. Furthermore, this superficial approach can lead to constant insecurity, as there will always be someone younger or more attractive than the current partner.

Personal value should not be tied solely to the characteristics of the partner, as this creates superficial relationships and unrealistic expectations that tend to fall apart over time.

The Mistake of Underestimating Emotional and Intellectual Compatibility

A crucial mistake in Hypergamous dynamics is the tendency to underestimate the importance of long-term emotional and intellectual compatibility. In both men and women, an exclusive focus on economic status, youth, or physical appearance can overshadow other factors essential to a successful and fulfilling relationship.

<u>Relationships based solely on economics:</u> Women who focus exclusively on finding a partner with greater resources may overlook essential factors such as shared values, communication, and emotional empathy. This can lead to cold or functional relationships that lack true connection. In the long term, these relationships can become unsustainable, as a lack of emotional compatibility can lead to resentment, tension, and an emotional disconnect.

<u>Relationships based solely on physical appearance</u>: Men who prioritize youth and beauty may fall into relationships where, although there is a strong initial attraction, they lack a solid intellectual and emotional foundation. Physical beauty is fleeting, and if there are no other strong foundations, the relationship can fall apart when appearance changes or expectations are not met.

Emotional and intellectual compatibility is crucial to the success of long-term relationships. Couples who understand each other and share interests, values, and a deep emotional connection often have a stronger foundation for facing the challenges that inevitably arise in life.

The Mistake of Believing Hypergamy Guarantees Relationship Success

Another common mistake in Hypergamous dynamics is the belief that strictly following Hypergamous patterns guarantees relationship success. Many people assume that if they meet the traditional criteria of Hypergamy—a woman seeking status and a man seeking beauty—they will have a successful and fulfilling relationship. However, this assumption fails to take into account the complexities of human relationships.

The "Providing = Happiness" Fallacy: Some women believe that if they find a man with high status and economic stability, everything else will automatically fall into place. However, material provision does not guarantee happiness or emotional satisfaction. Many relationships that appear to meet traditional Hypergamous requirements fail due to a lack of compatibility in other fundamental ways, such as communication, respect, and emotional support.

The "Beauty = Happiness" Fallacy: Similarly, some men assume that if they find an attractive, young woman, that will be enough to guarantee relationship success. However, as mentioned above, beauty is temporary, and relationships that are based solely on physical attractiveness tend to lose their spark as emotional dynamics and the difficulties of everyday life take over.

The belief that Hypergamy guarantees long-term success is a mistake, as relationships are more complex and multifaceted than these superficial patterns allow.

The Mistake of Ignoring Power and Control Dynamics

A major mistake in Hypergamous relationships is ignoring the power and control dynamics that can arise when one person has more resources, status, or influence than the other. These dynamics can throw relationships out of balance and lead to toxic patterns that undermine equality and mutual respect.

Economic Imbalance and Control: In a relationship where a man has significantly higher economic status, there may be a temptation to exert control or power over the woman. This can manifest itself in financial decisions, control over the partner's activities or friendships, or even in more subtle forms of emotional manipulation. Women who are financially dependent on their partner may feel trapped in the relationship, leading to resentment and long-term dysfunction.

Emotional Control Based on Appearance: On the other hand, men who focus on younger, more attractive women may try to exert control over their partner's appearance, which can lead to insecurities and unhealthy pressures. Power dynamics in Hypergamous relationships are often not balanced, creating an environment where manipulation or abuse can flourish.

Couples must recognize and address any power imbalances to foster an equitable and respectful relationship, rather than perpetuating dynamics of control and subordination.

The Mistake of Constant Competition

Finally, a common mistake in Hypergamous dynamics is living in constant competition. This mistake manifests itself in both men and women who feel they must always compete with other people to keep their partner or to improve their status in the relationship.

Competition between women: For women, competition can arise around seeking out high-status men or maintaining physical appearance to remain desirable. This can lead to strained relationships between women and foster rivalry, rather than promoting mutual support and healthy self-esteem. The pressure to constantly compete can wear on women, both emotionally and physically.

Competition between men: Men, on the other hand, can fall into a competition to obtain the youngest or most attractive women, which can lead to an endless cycle of comparison and seeking external validation. This perpetual competition can undermine trust and lead to shallow relationships, as the focus is on outward appearance rather than emotional connection or compatibility.

Hypergamous dynamics, while they may have deep biological and cultural roots, should not completely dictate the way we relate. It is crucial to avoid common mistakes associated with Hypergamy, such as idealizing one's partner, constant competition, or believing that strictly following these patterns guarantees success. By recognizing and balancing these dynamics, people can build healthier relationships, based on mutual respect, emotional compatibility, and growing together.

Chapter 5
Hypergamy in the Digital Age: Social Media and Dating Apps

The digital age has transformed interpersonal relationships, and with it, the dynamics of hypergamy have been greatly influenced. Social media and dating apps have facilitated interaction between people of different social, economic, and geographic statuses, allowing users to access a greater variety of potential partners. However, these platforms have also amplified certain hypergamous tendencies and introduced new challenges to relationships. In this chapter, we will explore how hypergamy manifests itself in the digital world and the effects that new technologies have had on the dynamics of attraction and partner selection.

Hypergamy Empowered by Access to Global Information

Before the advent of the internet and social media, interactions and relationship opportunities were limited to local social circles. With the advent of platforms such as Instagram, Facebook, Tinder, and Bumble, people's social reach has greatly expanded, providing access to individuals who would have previously been outside their geographic or social radar.

<u>Expansion of options:</u> In the context of hypergamy, this expansion means that people can "shop around" for potential partners on a global level. Both men and

women can observe and, in some cases, interact with individuals who belong to a social, economic, or physical elite, which fosters an environment in which people seek access to higher-status individuals. This reinforces hypergamous tendencies, where women, for example, seek out men with greater resources and men prioritize young, attractive women.

<u>"Hyperfocus" phenomenon of attention:</u> Dating apps have also facilitated what some experts call "hyperfocus" of attention toward a small group of highly attractive people. A study on Tinder, for example, found that a small percentage of men and women (approximately 20%) receive most interactions, while the rest are left with few options. This phenomenon is a direct reflection of hypergamous dynamics, where women look for the man with the highest status and men look for the younger, more attractive women. As a result, many people are excluded from interaction on these platforms, which generates frustration and anxiety. In turn, on these platforms, the most attractive women, who surely receive hundreds of male messages, could quickly select a potential romantic candidate and leave the application. Therefore, the platform bombards her with less "desirable" men so that she "stays hooked on the search."

The effects of social networks on the perception of personal value

Social networks have created an environment in which external validation has become a determining factor of self-esteem. The dynamics of hypergamy have been amplified by the constant bombardment of images of success, beauty, and luxury that predominate on platforms such as Instagram. This affects both men and women, but in different ways, exacerbating traditional hypergamous expectations.

<u>The pressure on women:</u> Women in particular face constant pressure to maintain an idealized physical image. On social media, women are bombarded with images of influencers, models, and celebrities displaying young, attractive bodies, creating an unrealistic standard of beauty. This constant comparison can lead to women feeling like they need to meet certain standards to be considered desirable, reinforcing the hypergamous dynamic where a woman's worth is measured based on her appearance.

<u>The pressure on men:</u> Similarly, men are exposed to images of material success – luxury cars, designer clothes, and an opulent lifestyle. This reinforces the idea that men must achieve a high economic and social status to be considered attractive. Men who fail to meet these standards may feel insecure and anxious about their worth, leading them to constantly compare themselves to others and seek validation through the accumulation of wealth or status.

The "Tinder Effect" and the Illusion of Infinite Options

Dating apps like Tinder, Bumble, and Hinge have revolutionized the way people search for partners. While these platforms promise to expand opportunities for interaction, they have also created an illusion of infinite options, which has profoundly altered the dynamics of attraction and partner choice.

<u>Devaluing One-on-One Interactions:</u> Because of the ease with which one can swipe left or right, many people view interactions on these apps as disposable. If a person doesn't meet all expectations right away, it's easy to simply move on to the next option. This attitude reinforces the search for a "perfect match" that fits hypergamous standards of status, beauty, and youth, but is often hard to find. Constantly searching for a better option can lead to shallow relationships or an inability to commit to someone long-term.

<u>Difficulty building deep relationships:</u> The abundance of options on dating apps can also make it difficult to form deep, meaningful relationships. Instead of investing time in getting to know a person and building an emotional connection, many people choose to keep looking, believing they will eventually find a better fit. This creates a cycle of fleeting relationships and the perception that there is always something better available, which can make it difficult to develop real, solid commitments.

The Algorithm and Hypergamy: How Platforms Reinforce Selective Tendencies

Dating apps are not neutral in their operation; they are designed to maximize user engagement, which means their algorithms tend to reinforce hypergamous dynamics. Through artificial intelligence and data analysis, platforms adjust which profiles they show each user based on their preferences and the past behaviors of other users.

<u>Prioritizing status and attractiveness:</u> Dating app algorithms tend to show profiles that have received more positive interactions first, which often means that higher-status men and more attractive women receive more visibility. This creates a feedback loop where these individuals get more "matches" and reinforces traditional hypergamous criteria for mate selection. As a result, many people are excluded from interaction because they do not meet the most popular standards, leading to frustration and feelings of rejection.

<u>Fostering superficiality:</u> By focusing on physical attractiveness and status achievements, these platforms promote superficial relationships. The ease with which users can filter and select partners based on photos or brief profile details reinforces the tendency to look for external attributes rather than prioritizing emotional or intellectual compatibility. This leads to a reductionist approach to mate-finding, which leaves out many important aspects of human relationships.

The Distortion of Reality on Social Media: Idealized Projections

On social media, both men and women project idealized versions of themselves. These platforms allow people to construct a carefully curated image, showing only the most attractive aspects of their lives, which can distort the perception of reality in both those who broadcast and those who consume this content.

The Illusion of Perfection: Images and posts on social media are designed to present a highly edited and positive version of people's lives. Women show toned bodies, youth, and flawless beauty, while men exhibit financial success, travel, and professional achievements. This carefully edited "reality" creates unrealistic expectations about what a perfect couple should be, perpetuating traditional Hypergamous ideals.

Destructive Comparisons: Seeing these idealized versions of others, many people fall into the trap of constantly comparing themselves. Women may feel pressured to meet the standards of beauty and youth they see in influencers and models (which are not exempt from being deceptive by the filters they use), while men may feel that they are not successful or powerful enough compared to others (who often display luxury items that do not belong to them). This constant comparison negatively affects self-esteem and personal security, leading to decisions in relationships that are not based on reality, but on an unattainable ideal.

Psychological Effects of Digital Hypergamy: Anxiety and Disillusionment

Constant exposure to elevated Hypergamous standards on social media and dating apps can have profound psychological effects on people. Both men and women can develop high levels of anxiety and frustration due to the pressure to meet Hypergamous expectations, often leading to disillusionment and disappointment.

<u>Anxiety in women about physical appearance:</u> Women who do not fit the beauty standards projected on social media may experience anxiety and low self-esteem. Constant comparison to models and influencers can lead to an obsession with physical appearance, driving excessive use of makeup, filters, or even surgical procedures to meet unrealistic standards of beauty. This anxiety about meeting the Hypergamous "ideal" can affect mental health and self-perception.

Women who only offer the exhibition of their bodies on social networks are people in need of validation, and only get approval from simple men, that is, from men who do not want anything serious with them. Women are more attractive in the eyes of men when they share photographs of their daily lives, demonstrating their social skills by reading a book, cooking, working in the garden, etc. Men value these customs and perceive them as long-term partners.

<u>Frustration in men due to status:</u> Men who do not reach the levels of success or power shown on social networks may feel frustrated or insufficient. This can generate constant competition to "prove" their value through the acquisition of wealth, professional success, or material goods. Frustration at not meeting hypergamous expectations can lead to low self-esteem, stress, and a superficial focus on finding a partner. Although a man in his 20s may be at a disadvantage with a man in his 30s, the truth is that men are built, so nothing is defined, but everything is to be seen and experienced.

The digital age has amplified hypergamous dynamics, but it has also created new opportunities and challenges for relationships. Social media and dating apps have transformed the way people connect, but they have also reinforced stereotypes and unrealistic expectations. To meet these challenges, people must develop a greater awareness of how technology affects their relationship decisions, avoiding falling into the trap of superficiality and cultivating relationships based on authenticity, emotional compatibility, and mutual respect.

Chapter 6
How to deal with hypergamy

At What Age Do Men and Women Become More Attractive and Valuable? A Research-Based Perspective

Attraction and perceived value between men and women change significantly with age, a phenomenon that has been the subject of study in the fields of evolutionary psychology, sociology, and dating dynamics analysis. While attractiveness is influenced by multiple individual factors, such as personality, intelligence, and humor, several studies have found clear patterns about at what age men and women tend to be more valued by the other gender, and the reasons behind these preferences.

Female Attraction and Youth

Studies on male preferences have shown a consistent pattern: men tend to be more attracted to younger women, especially in the age bracket between 18 and 25. A study conducted by OKCupid in 2010, based on millions of interactions on the platform, found that men of all ages tend to prefer women in their 20s, even if they are significantly older.

• Biological Reasons
From an evolutionary perspective, men are often attracted to female youth because it is an indicator of fertility and reproductive health. During the twenties,

women are generally at their peak fertility, which biologically makes them more attractive to men who are subconsciously looking for a partner with a high probability of conceiving.

Peak Fertility: Youth is directly associated with reproductive capacity, and evolutionary psychology studies suggest that this is one of the main reasons why men tend to be attracted to women in their twenties.

Physical Appearance: On an aesthetic level, young women often exhibit physical characteristics that are considered universally attractive: smooth skin, facial symmetry, and a body mass index that tends to approach classic beauty standards.

• **Social Factors**
While biology plays an important role, social factors also influence this perception. Younger women tend to be seen as more open to new experiences and more willing to start a family, which can be attractive to men looking for long-term relationships.

The Value of Men: Maturity and Stability

In contrast, studies show that male attractiveness in the eyes of women follows a different pattern. Men tend to value themselves more in their early adult years, whereas women are typically more attracted to men in their 30s and 40s. In the same OKCupid study, it was found that women, as they age, tend to prefer men who are older than them, and the most attractive men to women are generally in the 35-45 age range.

• Biological Reasons

From an evolutionary standpoint, women are typically attracted to men who can provide security and stability, which tends to correlate with age. Instead of focusing solely on physical appearance, women value more attributes related to the ability to provide resources, protection, and a stable environment.

Financial and Social Stability: Older men tend to have greater financial success and stability in their careers, which makes them more attractive to women seeking long-term stability, especially when it comes to starting a family.

Emotional Maturity: Emotional maturity and life experience are also factors valued by women in older men. The ability to deal with stress, make decisions, and handle complicated situations tends to improve with age, which increases the attractiveness of men. However, there are cases in which women abandon the "good guy" for the "bad and vicious" one, and it is because the second is not better than the first, but rather provides excitement, adventure, and a certain emotional instability that is seductive when the woman is young, and that the "good guy" in his eagerness to provide and respect all the rules, does not manage to generate.

• Social Factors

Older men tend to have greater clarity about what they are looking for in a relationship, which builds trust in women. In addition, the maturity and social status that men achieve over time increase their perceived value.

Changes in perceived value with age

For both men and women, attractiveness and perceived value are not static but fluctuate throughout life. Women tend to be valued more in their youth due to the biological reasons mentioned above, but as they age, the value that men place on them tends to decrease. However, women who focus on personal development, emotional intelligence, and their professional careers can compensate for this change, attracting men who value more aspects related to emotional connection and stability.

On the other hand, men tend to "improve" their attractiveness with age, especially between 30 and 50 years old. During this stage, men tend to reach their greatest economic and professional success, which gives them greater value in the eyes of women looking for stable and secure relationships.

While studies show clear patterns about the age at which men and women are considered most attractive, it is important to keep in mind that attraction is not just biological. Personal qualities, such as confidence, emotional intelligence, and the ability to genuinely connect, play an essential role in valuing a partner. Youth and stability are important factors, but satisfying relationships are based on deeper aspects than these superficial values.

In conclusion, both men and women can increase their value and attractiveness by focusing on personal growth, emotional intelligence, and general well-being, regardless of age.

How to become more attractive and valuable to the opposite sex according to the parameters of Hypergamy

Hypergamy, defined as the tendency to seek a partner at a higher rank in terms of status, attractiveness, or resources, has shaped the way men and women relate to and choose partners throughout history. Both men and women can increase their attractiveness and value to the opposite sex by following certain principles based on the Hypergamous nature of relationships.

In terms of Hypergamy, women tend to look for security, stability, and resources in a man. This is not limited to the economic aspect alone but encompasses a combination of qualities that reinforce a man's ability to offer a stable life and a promising future.

1. Improving Economic and Professional Status
One of the main factors that increase a man's value in the Hypergamous dynamic is his economic capacity. This does not imply that men must be millionaires, but having a stable career and being on an upward trajectory in their profession is attractive to many women, as it denotes security and the ability to provide. It must be remembered that, generally, economic stability is achieved from the age of 30, but at a younger age you can show that you are on the right path, showing interests, working on them and not lying on a couch playing PlayStation, or drinking beer like a bottomless barrel at every party you organize.

Professional Development: Investing in education and skills that will allow you to advance in your career is key. Men who show ambition, discipline, and success in their fields are perceived as more valuable. These factors not only increase economic status but also social status.

<u>Financial Security:</u> In addition to generating income, it is important to demonstrate financial intelligence, that is, knowing how to manage money, save, and invest in a solid future. This project's maturity and the ability to handle long-term responsibilities are qualities valued in a Hypergamous context.

2. Self-confidence and Leadership
In Hypergamous dynamics, self-confidence is one of the most attractive traits a man can possess. Women tend to be attracted to men who show leadership, assertiveness, and a positive attitude toward life. Therefore, the man should organize the dates, be the one to propose ideas and demonstrate firmness of character to the woman. This does not mean being arrogant, but rather feeling confident in one's own decisions, being able to take initiative, and assuming responsibility. Men who show self-confidence tend to be perceived as more capable of protecting and guiding, which fits with the traditional parameters of Hypergamy.

It is not necessary to be a leader in all facets of life, but being someone who makes decisions, acts decisively, and shows skills to lead in difficult situations increases male attractiveness. Leadership is closely linked to social status and control of resources.

3. Health and Personal Care
Physical appearance is still important, although it is not necessarily the predominant factor for men in

Hypergamous dynamics. However, a man who takes care of himself is fit and displays healthy lifestyle habits, is more attractive because he projects vitality, self-control, and discipline.

Staying fit and taking care of one's health not only improves physical appearance but also conveys that the man is disciplined and committed to his well-being. This reflects a subconscious level that will be able to take care of others.

Dressing well and having a neat appearance also play an important role. Men who take care of their image are perceived as more attractive because they show that they understand the value of impressions and self-care.

How to Increase Attractiveness in Women: Beauty and Femininity

For women, Hypergamy suggests that youth, beauty, and femininity are key factors in the attraction felt by men. However, this does not mean that women must comply with rigid stereotypes; Rather, it is about optimizing and enhancing the attributes that are normally valued.

1. Beauty and physical health

Physical attractiveness is one of the most prominent characteristics in the parameters of hypergamy when it comes to male attraction. Men tend to be attracted to women who project youth and health, as these are biological indicators of fertility.

<u>Skincare and physical appearance:</u> Maintaining healthy and radiant skin, as well as a fit body, are aspects that increase physical attraction. This does not imply that all women must conform to a single standard of beauty, but it is beneficial to take care of physical appearance in a way that highlights health and vitality.

<u>Personal style and femininity:</u> Femininity does not refer exclusively to traditional gender standards but to the ability to enhance attributes that project delicacy and physical attraction. Dressing elegantly and taking care of personal presentation can considerably increase male attraction. The woman should not imitate the man, but rather be his opposite, the counterpart that the man needs to be complete. A masculine woman does not attract, she is only positioned as a friend of the man.

2. Emotional Intelligence and Support

Although physical beauty is an important factor, many men also look for emotional connection and support in a partner. Emotional intelligence is an attribute that women can develop to strengthen their relationships and attract potential partners.

<u>Ability to nurture relationships:</u> Being understanding, empathetic, and emotionally stable is an attribute highly valued by men. A woman who knows how to manage conflict, who supports her partner in his goals,

and who fosters a deep emotional connection tends to be more attractive for long-term relationships.

<u>Assertive communication:</u> Women who can express their emotions clearly and positively without being confrontational have an advantage in relationships. Men value women who can solve problems constructively and who foster an environment of peace and support.

3. Authenticity and self-confidence

Confidence is one of the most attractive traits in any person, and women who project authenticity and self-confidence capture the attention of men.

<u>Security and self-esteem:</u> A woman who feels comfortable with herself and does not need constant validation is seen as more attractive. Self-confidence is not only reflected in the way she relates to others but also in how she projects herself on a personal and professional level.

<u>Check your social media posts:</u> If you only post scantily clad photos, in provocative poses, you are surely seeking male approval; but you will only get the attention of mediocre men who only see you as an object, and not for what you are worth. You will never get a man of great value as a life partner.

<u>Authenticity in femininity:</u> Being authentic and not trying to conform to an ideal or image that is not real is highly valued by men. A woman who is genuine and comfortable with her own identity, instead of trying to conform to external expectations, is more attractive.

The Value of Both Genders in Modern Hypergamy

Although traditional Hypergamy may seem based on material and superficial aspects, relationships today demand something more. Power dynamics between genders have evolved and both men and women can excel through personal development, emotional growth, and continuous improvement.

1. Enriching Emotional Connection
Aside from the factors mentioned, both men and women can increase their value by developing emotional communication skills and empathy. These aspects are fundamental to strengthening long-term relationships and creating a connection that goes beyond the physical or material.

2. Personal Growth and Adaptability
In a constantly changing world, the most attractive people are those who show personal growth and the ability to adapt. Women who strive to grow intellectually and emotionally, and men who dedicate themselves to developing their emotional intelligence and improving their status, are not only more attractive but are also able to maintain more satisfying and balanced relationships.

Hypergamy therefore sets certain traditional parameters on attraction between men and women, but these can be understood and applied in a healthy way to optimize the quality of relationships. Both men and women can become more attractive and valuable to the opposite sex by investing in their personal development, taking care of their physical appearance, improving their emotional skills, and communicating effectively. These efforts will not only increase their perceived value, but will also allow them to create deeper, more meaningful, and more balanced relationships.

Understanding the traditional parameters of Hypergamy, when approached with a modern and healthy perspective, can allow both men and women to develop greater awareness of themselves and their relationships. It is not just about meeting expectations based on status or beauty, but about evolving as individuals in all areas of life. Personal growth, self-confidence, and emotional intelligence are critical to cultivating authentic and meaningful relationships.

Reflection on Hypergamy in the Current Context

Although Hypergamous parameters are deeply rooted in biology and evolution, in contemporary society, relationships are no longer based exclusively on traditional gender roles. Women have gained economic independence and men value emotional connection more than mere appearances. However, aspects such as security, stability, and physical attractiveness remain important for both genders, although in a balanced and flexible way.

For men, the value they can offer in a relationship goes beyond economic resources; emotional intelligence, leadership ability, and self-confidence are equally important to attract and maintain a quality relationship.

For women, although physical beauty remains an attractive key, true value is reflected in their emotional intelligence, support, and ability to nurture relationships from a genuine and equal perspective.

Practical advice for both genders

<u>Personal development:</u> Continuing to learn, improve in one's professional career, and take care of one's mental and emotional health increases the value of any individual in a relationship.

<u>Physical Self-Care:</u> Physical health and well-being are essential. Staying fit and healthy not only improves your appearance but also boosts your self-confidence.

<u>Emotional Intelligence:</u> Developing the ability to understand, express, and manage emotions is vital for emotional connection and building lasting relationships.

<u>Authenticity:</u> Being genuine and not trying to conform to external expectations is key to attracting a partner who values who you are at your core.

<u>Effective Communication:</u> Learning to communicate openly and assertively fosters healthier relationships and reduces misunderstandings.

Becoming more attractive and valuable to the opposite sex doesn't mean conforming to unattainable or superficial ideals. It's about investing in yourself, both physically and emotionally, and projecting an image that reflects security, empathy, and authenticity. By improving in these areas, men and women not only optimize their value within traditional Hypergamous parameters, but they are also better equipped to create deeper, more fulfilling relationships in an increasingly complex world.

The man is always at a disadvantage

It is well known that men are born with a disadvantage. On the other hand, women are perceived from birth as weak beings who must be cared for, and who are allowed to express their feelings of vulnerability; while the little boy is called to be a MAN and not to cry, and who must always protect the woman at all costs.

With the arrival of adolescence, women do not have to do anything, they already bring with them the elements to attract attention, while men must build themselves, educate themselves, and mature to be able to seduce and be chosen. While women will reject left and right, because they never lack suitors, men must learn from rejections and understand that they are in an eternal competition with other men who are more valuable than them, and who are the ones who get the girls.

Below, we can highlight several aspects of male behavior that are key to maintaining a healthy relationship and avoiding falling into patterns that lead to failure or loss of respect in the couple. Below, we analyze the most outstanding points:

1. Avoid "Simp" Behavior

One of the recurring themes in the life of the growing man is to avoid falling into the dynamics of what is called "simp" or "creepy" behavior. This term refers to men who are excessively accommodating, helpful, or submissive to win a woman's affection, losing their dignity and personal value in the process.

A man who is always available, who puts his partner on a pedestal, or who is emotionally dependent on her approval, will inevitably lose his attractiveness in the long term. The man must maintain his individuality, his dignity, and his own life, without falling into attitudes that devalue him.

2. The Value of Self-Sufficiency

It must be firm in pointing out that men must be emotionally and financially self-sufficient. Dependency, both financial and emotional, is seen as a weakness that can deteriorate a relationship.

<u>Emotional Independence:</u> Men should not base their happiness or self-esteem exclusively on their relationship with their partner. An emotionally self-sufficient man is more attractive because he doesn't need to be constantly validated by his partner to feel good.

<u>Financial independence:</u> Having a stable and well-managed professional life is essential. This not only gives confidence but reinforces the feeling of control over life, which is crucial in the dynamics of attraction.

3. Maintaining Emotional Control

One of the fundamental pillars of healthy masculinity is that men must learn to control their emotions, especially when it comes to conflicts or breakups. Showing desperation, insecurity, or excessive anger in difficult times undermines attraction and the partner's respect.

Handling breakups: The most prominent recommendation is not to beg, not to pursue, and not to show emotional weakness in front of the ex-partner. This approach, known as the "law of ice", advocates total distancing after a breakup, allowing the man to regain his dignity and, in many cases, increasing the likelihood that the woman will value him again.

Avoid emotional reactivity: Men should avoid being reactive to emotional provocations or manipulations. Staying calm and projecting confidence in times of tension helps preserve respect and attraction within the relationship.

4. Be the leader in the relationship

Men should occupy a leadership position within the relationship, but this does not mean being authoritarian or controlling. Rather, it refers to the fact that men should be clear about what they want, make decisions, and act proactively.

Security and direction: A man who knows what he wants and can make decisions shows an attractive quality for women. Indecision or dependence on the opinion of his partner for every detail of the relationship can lead to a woman losing interest or respect.

Initiative: Men should not expect women to guide them in the relationship but should be the ones to push the direction and define the limits of what they want. This position is not sexist but rather seeks to get men to act with conviction and direction, two highly valued characteristics in romantic dynamics.

5. Respect personal space

Another important point is the importance of respecting personal space within the relationship. This includes maintaining a balance between time as a couple and individual activities. Excessive dependence and lack of a life of one's own outside the relationship are destructive.

Maintain hobbies and friendships: A man who does not abandon his passions, interests, and social circles for the relationship is more attractive, as he maintains an identity outside of the couple. When a man loses his individuality completely, he not only becomes less interesting but increases the likelihood that the relationship will become monotonous.

Letting the partner miss you: It is healthy for a woman to miss the man. Being available all the time or saturating the relationship with constant attention can wear down attraction. Giving space and respecting distance at certain times reinforces desire.

6. Avoid Idealizing the Partner

One of the most common mistakes men make is the tendency to idealize their partner, especially in the initial stages or after a breakup. This idealization can lead to emotional dependence and loss of a sense of reality.

Demystifying the relationship: Men are advised to focus on seeing the woman as a human being with flaws and virtues, rather than placing her on a pedestal. Idealizing a woman can lead to unrealistic expectations and, when these are not met, to frustration that affects the dynamics of the relationship.

Realism about the partner: Men must be realistic about who their partner is, not overvalue their role in the relationship, and always maintain their individuality and autonomy. By seeing your partner realistically, you avoid complacent and servile behaviors that often undermine respect and attraction.

7. Don't lose your purpose

One of the crucial points that is highlighted is that men should not lose sight of their purpose in life, regardless of their love situation. This is essential to maintain respect and admiration within a relationship.

Focus on goals and ambitions: A man who is focused on his personal goals and projects is more attractive. A man should not sacrifice his professional, personal, or emotional growth for a relationship, as this will eventually affect his self-esteem and, therefore, the dynamic with his partner.

Avoid emotional codependency: A warning is given against the risk of becoming too emotionally dependent on his partner. When a man puts his partner as the absolute center of his life and abandons his interests, he loses the power of attraction and creates an imbalance in the relationship.

8. The importance of knowing how to say No

The importance of men knowing how to set boundaries and say "no" when necessary is stressed. This point is fundamental to knowing how to maintain dignity and respect in a relationship.

Establish clear boundaries: Knowing how to say "no" is not only a matter of avoiding unnecessary complacency but also of establishing healthy boundaries in the relationship. A man who is not afraid to stand his ground and defend what he considers fair and necessary is seen as more respectable.

Avoid submission: Men who allow their partner to cross boundaries for fear of losing her are criticized. Submissive and accommodating behavior tends to generate contempt rather than affection, so knowing when to set boundaries and acting firmly is key to maintaining a balanced relationship.

9. The Law of Ice in Breakups

The Law of Ice is a method to handle breakups. After a breakup, men are advised to proceed to completely cut off contact with their ex-partner. This includes not texting, not trying to get her back, and essentially disappearing from her life completely for a while (or permanently).

<u>Regaining dignity</u>: This approach seeks to get the man to regain his dignity, control his emotions, and avoid appearing as someone desperate to get back together. By disappearing from his ex's radar, he allows her to value him from a distance, increasing the chance that she will be the one to seek contact again.

<u>Emotional recovery</u>: It is also emphasized that the Law of Ice is not only a strategy to win back the ex-partner, but a tool for the man to regain his emotional stability and focus on himself.

10. Understanding Female Psychology

It is stressed that it is important for men to understand some basic aspects of female psychology, especially regarding attraction and respect. Women, in general, do not value men who are too dependent or insecure and prefer those who stand firm and have a life of their own.

<u>Mystery and challenge</u>: One of the keys to maintaining a woman's interest is to maintain a certain level of mystery and challenge. Men who are always available and who do not present any challenge tend to lose their attractiveness more quickly.

<u>Avoid emotional excesses</u>: Although emotional intelligence is important, being too emotional or sensitive in front of a woman can lead to a loss of respect and attraction since this is often perceived as a sign of weakness.

70

This clear and direct approach to male behavior in relationships, based on self-sufficiency, emotional control, and self-respect, outlines how men should avoid falling into overindulgence or emotional dependence, and instead cultivate their individuality, ambition, and personal dignity. By following these principles, men will not only be able to maintain more balanced and satisfying relationships, but also avoid the common mistakes that lead to loss of respect and attraction in their partner.

Chapter 7
Beyond Hypergamy:
Relationships based on equality

Hypergamy, in both men and women, has been a key dynamic in mate choice throughout history, driven by biological and sociocultural factors. However, in recent decades, a significant shift has emerged in how people understand and value their relationships, prioritizing equality, emotional compatibility, and mutual respect over traditional patterns of status and attractiveness. This final chapter explores how relationships can move beyond hypergamous dynamics to build healthier and more equitable connections.

The Challenge of Overcoming Hypergamous Patterns

Overcoming hypergamous dynamics is not easy, as they are deeply rooted in our biology and culture. However, the growing movement toward gender equality, the transformation of traditional roles, and increased access to education and financial autonomy for women have facilitated an evolution toward more balanced relationships.

<u>Women's Financial Autonomy:</u> As more women gain access to education and economic independence, the need to seek a partner who will provide financial security has diminished. This has allowed women to focus their partner's decisions on factors such as emotional compatibility, shared interests, and equality

of values, rather than basing them primarily on the man's economic status.

<u>Changing expectations in men:</u> Men are also experiencing a change in their expectations of a partner. Instead of looking solely for young, attractive women, many men value their partner's intelligence, emotional support, and ability to be an equal partner. This shift reflects a move away from traditional Hypergamous expectations and a greater appreciation for long-term compatibility.

Equality-Based Relationships: Key Characteristics

Equality-based relationships focus on mutual respect, collaboration, and growing together. Below are some of the key characteristics that define this type of relationship.

Mutual Respect: In an equal relationship, both people respect each other's opinions, wants, and needs. It is not about one person having more power or control over the other, but about both individuals valuing and appreciating the other's qualities and recognizing their equality as partners.

<u>Collaboration and Support:</u> Relationships based on equality promote collaboration. Both men and women work together to achieve common goals, such as financial stability, emotional growth, and family well-being. Instead of focusing on traditional gender roles, both parties take on shared responsibilities, and one's success is seen as a joint success.

Emotional Compatibility: In these types of relationships, emotional connection takes priority over superficial expectations of status or beauty. The ability to communicate openly, understand each other's emotions, and support each other in times of difficulty are the pillars of a healthy and equitable relationship.

Equal Roles and Responsibilities: Equal relationships challenge traditional notions of gender roles, in which women take care of the home and men provide. Today, many couples choose to divide responsibilities equally, making decisions based on individual abilities and preferences, not societal expectations.

The Role of Feminism and the Gender Equality Movement

The feminist movement has played a crucial role in transforming relationships. Through the fight for equal rights and gender equity, women have gained more freedom to choose their partners based on their personal preferences rather than material needs. This has driven a cultural shift in how people perceive relationships.

Demystifying financial dependence: Before the advancement of women's rights, many relationships were founded on women's need to be economically dependent on men. With women's growing economic independence, traditional hypergamous dynamics have begun to lose their force. Women are no longer forced to choose partners based on their ability to provide, opening the door to more genuine, compatibility-focused relationships.

<u>New expectations for men:</u> Feminism has not only benefited women but has also allowed men to break free from traditional roles. Men in egalitarian relationships may feel less pressure to meet expectations of being the "provider" or proving their worth through economic achievements. Instead, they can focus on being emotionally present and responsible partners, which enriches the relationship.

The Impact of Technology on Hypergamy

In the contemporary context, technology has transformed relationship dynamics, influencing the practice of Hypergamy. With increased global connectivity, people are more likely to form cross-cultural couples, leading to a redefinition of Hypergamous relationships that prioritize shared experiences and lifestyle compatibility over traditional status markers.

This evolution reflects changing societal values and the increasing importance of adaptability and mutual growth in romantic relationships.

Communication as a Pillar of Equality

Communication is one of the most powerful tools for building and maintaining relationships based on equality. Instead of imposing unspoken expectations or following cultural norms without question, couples in equal relationships practice open and honest communication as a foundational pillar.

<u>Active listening and empathy:</u> In a relationship based on equality, both parties feel valued and heard. Active listening involves not only hearing what the other person says but also trying to understand their emotions and perspectives. Empathy is key to creating a space where both can express themselves without fear of judgment or criticism.

<u>Negotiation and conflict resolution:</u> Equal relationships require that both partners be willing to negotiate and resolve conflicts fairly. It's not about imposing one's will on the other, but about finding solutions that benefit both parties. This requires flexibility, understanding, and a willingness to compromise when necessary.

<u>Transparency in expectations and goals:</u> Couples who aspire to equal relationships are transparent about their expectations and goals. This includes everything from finances to responsibilities at home to future projects. Clarity and honesty in these areas prevent misunderstandings and ensure that both parties are working toward the same goals.

Challenges of Equal Relationships

Despite the advantages of relationships based on equality, they also face unique challenges. Equality does not happen automatically; it must be continually negotiated and cultivated. Some of the most common obstacles include:

<u>Income inequality:</u> Although economic independence is a key factor in equal relationships, many couples face differences in their income levels. This can lead to tensions if not addressed with open communication and clear agreements about how to handle finances.

<u>Cultural and social expectations:</u> Despite advances in gender equality, many societies still maintain traditional expectations about the roles of men and women. Couples who challenge these norms may face criticism or external pressure, which can make it difficult to create a truly equal relationship.

<u>Difficulty balancing careers and family responsibilities:</u> In an egalitarian relationship, both partners often want to succeed in their careers, which can create difficulties in balancing work and family responsibilities. This challenge requires careful planning and a willingness to share household and child-rearing responsibilities.

The Future of Equal Relationships

Not only do relationships based on equality represent a significant cultural shift, but they also offer a hopeful vision for the future of couples. As social norms continue to evolve and people seek more authentic and meaningful relationships, equal dynamics will likely continue to gain ground.

Historically, hypergamy served as a practical strategy for financial security, particularly for women in societies where economic opportunities were limited. However, the modern landscape has changed dramatically. With increased access to education and lucrative careers for women, financial independence has reduced dependence on a partner's wealth, allowing people to prioritize emotional and intellectual compatibility over mere economic status.

<u>The Importance of Growing Together:</u> Equal relationships are built on the idea that both individuals are committed to personal growth and mutual support. This approach allows couples to not only share their lives but also help each other achieve their individual goals.

<u>Flexibility in roles:</u> As societies move away from traditional gender expectations, couples will have more freedom to define their roles and responsibilities. This flexibility will allow relationships to adapt to changing life circumstances, strengthening emotional connection and promoting greater resilience in the couple.

<u>Intellectual compatibility:</u> Intellectual compatibility highlights the alignment of a couple's intellectual thoughts, interests, and goals. It involves engaging in stimulating conversations, challenging each other's viewpoints, and growing together. This aspect has gained importance in modern relationships as emotional and intellectual compatibility is increasingly seen as vital to longevity and satisfaction.

As people seek partners who resonate with their intellectual wavelengths, this shift reflects a more holistic approach to mate selection beyond traditional status markers.

<u>Changing gender roles</u>: As traditional gender roles continue to transform, Hypergamy has increasingly become a two-way street. Men are also considering things beyond financial status, such as emotional support and shared values. This shift reflects a broader movement toward egalitarian relationships, where both partners contribute and share financial responsibilities, redefining what it means to "marry someone of a higher status."

Ending

Hypergamy is the practice of seeking a partner from a higher socioeconomic status, traditionally characterized by "marriage of women from a higher socioeconomic status." This phenomenon has deep historical roots in societies governed by caste and class structures, where marriage was a crucial means of social mobility. As economic opportunities have evolved, particularly for women, the relevance of hypergamy has changed, leading to contemporary debates about its implications for modern relationships. Scholars highlight that hypergamy is not limited solely to economic gain; it also encompasses emotional compatibility and shared values, reflecting evolving gender dynamics and societal expectations.

The concept of hypergamy has generated both support and criticism. Proponents argue that it allows people to pursue fulfilling relationships that are aligned with their aspirations, challenging traditional gender roles. In contrast, critics argue that Hypergamy reinforces outdated stereotypes, which portray women as primarily motivated by financial security and undermine their autonomy. This polarized debate often leads to broader discussions about the nature of relationships and the influence of social norms on partner selection.

Recent studies indicate that Hypergamous behaviors are shaped by cultural influences and technological advances, such as the rise of online dating platforms. These tools allow people to connect with a wide range of potential partners, often prioritizing educational and professional attributes alongside financial considerations. This evolution highlights the ongoing complexity of Hypergamous dynamics in contemporary society, where motivations can vary widely depending on cultural context and individual aspirations.

At its core, Hypergamy remains a multifaceted issue that encompasses not only the pursuit of higher social status through marriage but also reflects broader societal changes and personal choices in the realm of romantic relationships. Their exploration opens avenues for understanding how relationships adapt to the changing economic, cultural, and technological landscapes of the 21st century.

Although hypergamy has been a dominant force in human relationships, the growth of equality-based relationships offers a healthier, more balanced alternative. These relationships are centered on mutual respect, open communication, and joint growth. While they face challenges, the potential for creating deeper, more meaningful relationships is undeniable. By letting go of traditional patterns of power and status, couples can build an authentic connection that prioritizes equality, emotional compatibility, and shared well-being.

_______0_______